Written and Illustrated by
Walter S. Crane IV

Most of the following pages were originally printed
in the first seven issues of **SHEBA,** ©1996 - 1998.

This collection © 2000 Walter S. Crane IV

Published by Sick Mind Press
PO Box 400602
N. Cambridge, MA 02140
www.shebacomic.com

Printed in Canada
First printing, June 2000

ISBN  0-9701814-0-X

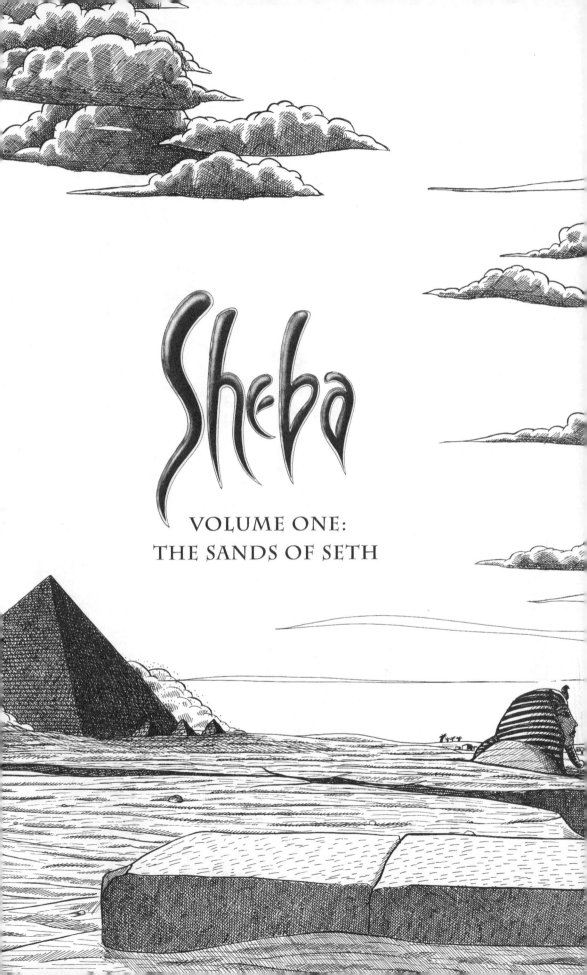

ONCE WE HAD IT MADE..
WE WERE GODS! WE WERE
WORSHIPPED, AND WE HAD **CULTURE**!

...NOW NO ONE REMEMBERS, OR CARES...

...MAKES ME WISH I WEREN'T IMMORTAL...

What's in that case? Not something DEAD, I hope...
QUIT WHINING! DO YOU WANT TO BE RICH, OR WHAT?!
SEE... MORE GOLD! NOTHING TO WORRY ABOUT...
CAN WE HURRY UP? I SWEAR THERE'S SOMETHING IN HERE!
YOU! HAVE! VIOLATED! TCH MY! HOLY! CHUCKLE TOMB!! PREPARE! TCH TO! DIE! CHUCKLE
THIS PLACE IS CURSED!!
NO! THAT WAS JUST ME AGAIN... MAN! YOU'RE SOOOO GULLIBLE!!!
uh... uh...

BRUSH, BRUSH
YAWN!!
WHO ARE YOU?
I'm your "Ba", -your spirit-
MY SPIRIT? ...THEN I'M DEAD, AND THIS IS THE AFTERLIFE...
..IS ALL THIS STUFF MINE?-EVERYTHING I'LL NEED, NOW THAT I'M GONE?

..A DISSATISFIED CUSTOMER!!

UH.. YOU MUST HAVE THE WRONG JACKAL-HEADED DEITY...

YOU'RE ANUBIS, GREAT GOD OF THE UNDERWORLD!

HEY, I'LL BE ANYBODY YOU WANT ME TO BE... RIGHT NOW I'M BUSY..

DOING WHAT?

I DON'T KNOW! LOOK, JUST GO AWAY! ...BESIDES.. I QUIT THAT GOD JOB A LONG TIME AGO!!

YOU'RE ANUBIS, AND YOU STILL HAVE A RESPONSIBILITY!

WHAT WAS THAT??
Oh, just a thing I do...
LEAP!
It appears these Arabs are more cunning than I had estimated..
ZWAP!
No matter...
SO! WHAT HAVE WE HERE?..MEDDLERS??
DO YOU THINK YOU CAN THWART MY EVIL PLAN??
WHAT "EVIL PLAN"?

WHAP!

WHERE'S THE DEMON KNOWN AS "ANUBIS"?

All those demons back there, like you, demon.
DEMON?? I'M ANUBIS GUARDIAN OF THE DEAD AND GOD OF MUMMIFICATION!!
GOD?!? But there is just one God, and His name is ALLAH!!
... Oh... You're ISLAMIC... That explains everything...

HEY! I'M BURAQ, AND I TOOK MOHAMMED TO SEE ALLAH!!
Yep.. yudda.. whatever... Excuse me, but I've got work to do here...
GEEZ! WHAT A MESS! IF I EVER SEE THOTH AGAIN, I'LL WRING HIM BY HIS SKINNY IBIS NECK!
WHAT'S A THOTH?

NOW MY SPHINX, WE SHALL STRIKE A BLOW FOR **OUR** EGYPT!!
AND THIS TIME, THERE WILL BE NO MORE DELAYS! NO MEDDLING MUMMIES OR FLYING HYBRID-THINGS!
BY DAWN'S LIGHT, YOU CAN HAVE ALL THE SARACENS YOU CAN EAT!!!

SLEEP WELL CAMPERS, FOR IT WILL BE AN ETERNAL SLUMBER!!
ANUBIS?
Uh.. Hi Seth... What's happening up here?
IT'S THE BEST PLACE TO SAVOR MY UPCOMING VICTORY!
I KNOW KHUFU'S PYRAMID IS BIGGER, BUT I DIDN'T WANT TO INSULT THE GREAT SPHINX!

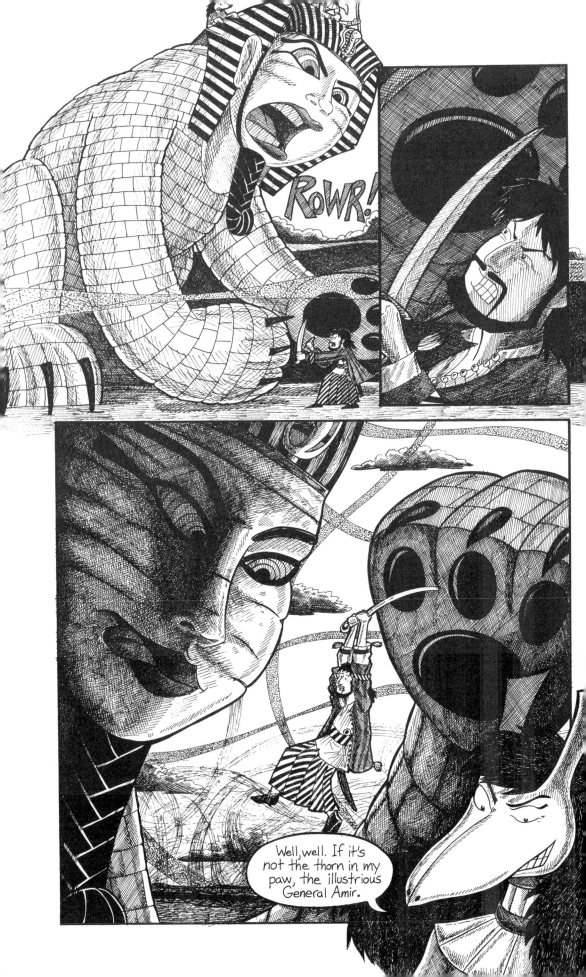

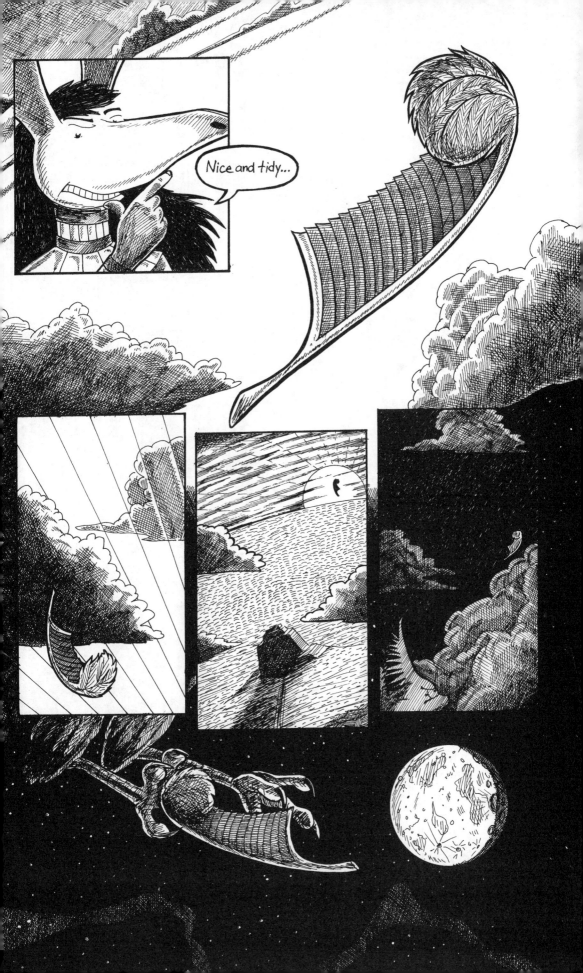

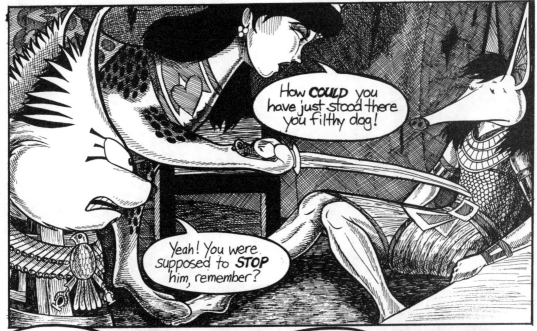

How **COULD** you have just stood there you filthy dog!

Yeah! You were supposed to **STOP** him, remember?

I only *said* I'd get the feather of Ma'at back!

But thanks to **YOU**, it's lost again!!

Hey! Don't you try to change the subject here!

Why didn't you fight Seth head to head??

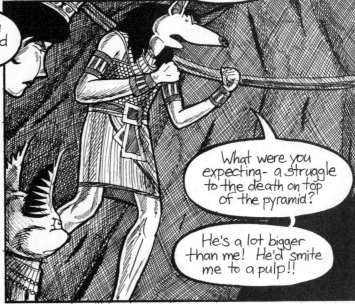

What were you expecting- a struggle to the death on top of the pyramid?

He's a lot bigger than me! He'd smite me to a pulp!!

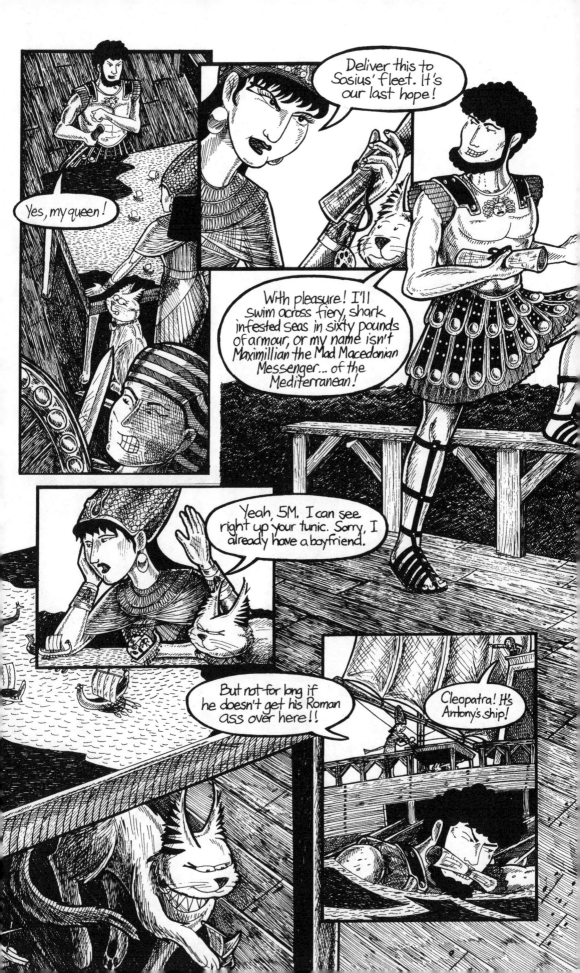

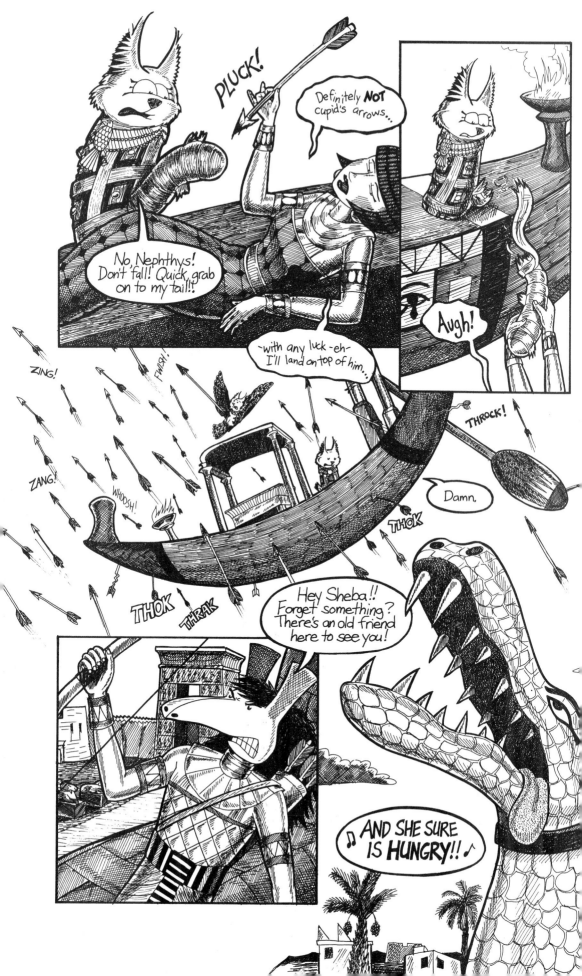

Ooo. **That** was low.

Fine. BE that way. Forget that we took you in when they all were sick of your scheming.. Just leave us here to wither.

Oh. You'll be fine.

Besides, how often am I asked to meddle?

Oh. Look. There's another one...

...Alexander the Great dropped these coins everywhere, way back when he tried to take over the known world...

Iskandar?*

But the world was much bigger than he thought.

It was here that the Macedonian gave up, thinking only ocean lay beyond India...

And like your people, his intentions were good. But he came up against the resolve of these people...

Never knowing what lay beyond. So many distant lands with so many gods.

- Not lands of a distant god.

...won't they?

But everyone can be at peace if they just submit to Allah!

Come on inside... I'll keep the "demons" at bay for you.

* Iskandar is the Arabic name for Alexander, who is revered in Islamic legend. Buraq knows this, and now you do too!

CONTINUED
IN

*Sheba*

VOLUME
TWO

And now, from the 13th nome of Egypt comes the tale of the #1 gnome of Egypt!

# The "Bes" Defense

The streets of Heliopolis, a sleepy Delta town, 1180 B.C.E.

Here we follow the nocturnal wanderings of Neferet, a young mother-to-be, on a beautiful Egyptian night.

Just the sort of night for a leisurely stroll down the Nile...

What a beautiful night for a stroll!!

Oof. Someone else is taking a stroll of their own.

But this same night also conceals a silent-running threat—

Kick!

the Sea Peoples!